A Beginning-to-Read Book

Winter

by Mary Lindeen

NORWOOD HOUSE PRESS

DEAR CAREGIVER,

The *Beginning to Read—Read and Discover* books provide emergent readers the opportunity to explore the world through nonfiction while building early reading skills. The text integrates both common sight words and content vocabulary. These key words are featured on lists provided at the back of the book to help your child expand his or her sight word recognition, which helps build reading fluency. The content words expand vocabulary and support comprehension.

Nonfiction text is any text that is factual. The Common Core State Standards call for an increase in the amount of informational text reading among students. The Standards aim to promote college and career readiness among students. Preparation for college and career endeavors requires proficiency in reading complex informational texts in a variety of content areas. You can help your child build a foundation by introducing nonfiction early. To further support the CCSS, you will find Reading Reinforcement activities at the back of the book that are aligned to these Standards.

Above all, the most important part of the reading experience is to have fun and enjoy it!

Sincerely,

Shannon Cannon

Shannon Cannon, Ph.D.
Literacy Consultant

Norwood House Press • P.O. Box 316598 • Chicago, Illinois 60631
For more information about Norwood House Press please visit our website at
www.norwoodhousepress.com or call 866-565-2900.
© 2016 Norwood House Press. Beginning-to-Read™ is a trademark of Norwood House Press.
All rights reserved. No part of this book may be reproduced or utilized in any form or by any
means without written permission from the publisher.

Editor: Judy Kentor Schmauss
Designer: Lindaanne Donohoe

Photo Credits:

Shutterstock, cover, 1, 4-5, 8-9, 18-19, 24-25; Dreamstime, 22-23, 28-29; iStock, 26-27;
Phil Martin, 3, 6-7, 10, 11, 12-13, 14-15, 16, 17, 20-21

Library of Congress Cataloging-in-Publication Data
   Lindeen, Mary, author.
    Winter / by Mary Lindeen.
       pages cm. – (A beginning to read book)
    Summary: "Winter is a special time of year. The air is cold, snow falls, and animals sleep.
 People go sledding and skating and celebrate New Year's Day and Valentine's Day.
 Find out about all the things there are to do in winter. This title includes reading activities
 and a word list"– Provided by publisher.
    Audience: Grades K to 3.
    ISBN 978-1-59953-682-8 (library edition : alk. paper)
    ISBN 978-1-60357-767-0 (ebook)
    1. Winter–Juvenile literature. 2. Snow–Juvenile literature. I. Title.
    QB637.8.L56 2015
    508.2–dc23
                                                        2014047621

Manufactured in the United States of America in Stevens Point, Wisconsin. 275N–062015

It is winter.

Winter comes after fall.

The air gets cold in the winter.

You can see frost.

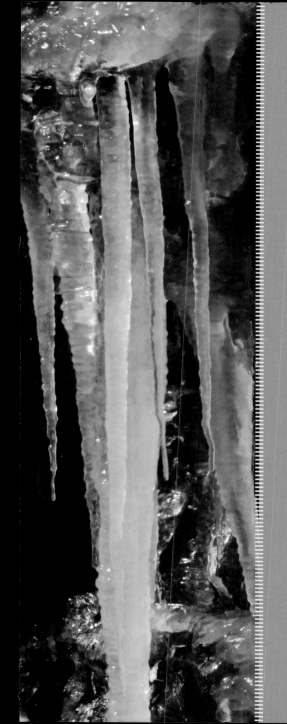

Icicles hang down.

It snows and snows.

Snow can be a lot
of work.

Snow can be fun, too.
Put on your warm clothes.

Now you can go out!

You can play
in the snow.

You can make
a snowman.

You can go sledding.

Whoosh! Whoosh!

These people are ice skating.

Try not to fall!

Trees do not grow
in winter.

Where are their
leaves?

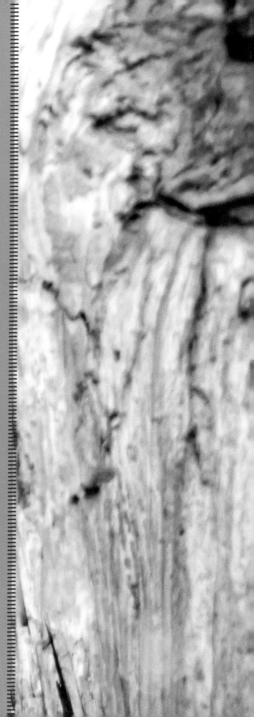

Animals must stay warm, too.

This animal's home is warm.

Some animals
sleep all winter.

This animal will
wake up in the
spring.

New Year's Day
is in the winter.

It is the first day
of the new year.

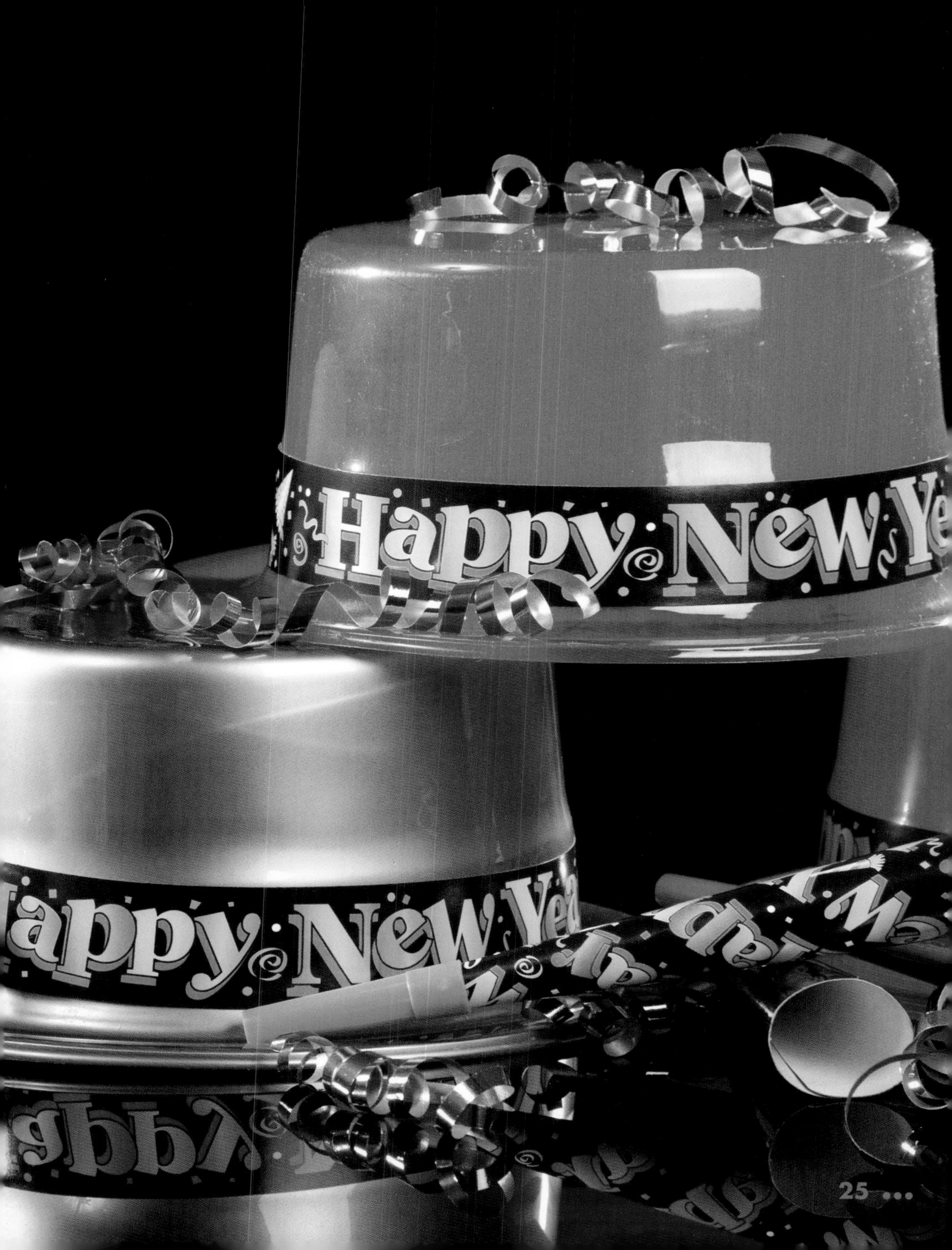
Happy New Ye
appy New Yea

Valentine's Day
is another special
winter day.

Some people give
and get gifts or
cards.

There are many things to do in the winter.

What do you like to do?

·· **Reading Reinforcement** ··

CRAFT AND STRUCTURE

To check your child's understanding of this book, recreate the following diagram on a sheet of paper. Read the book with your child, then help him or her fill in the diagram using what they learned. Work together to complete the diagram by writing words or ideas from this text that connect with the senses:

See	Touch	Hear
Smell	Taste	Feel

VOCABULARY: Learning Content Words

Content words are words that are specific to a particular topic. All of the content words for this book can be found on page 32. Use some or all of these content words to complete one or more of the following activities:

• Create a word web for one or more of the content words. Write the word itself in the center of the web, and synonyms (words with similar meanings), antonyms (words with opposite meanings), or other related words in the outer spokes.

• Have your child identify a content word by using three clues you provide; for example, *hat, coat, gloves* → *clothes.*

• Say a content word and have your child act out its meaning.

• Write the content words on slips of paper. Place them in a box. Have your child pick a word and use it in a sentence.

• Help your child find pictures in magazines that remind him or her of the meaning of a content word. Cut out the pictures, and use them to make a page for a picture dictionary.

FOUNDATIONAL SKILLS: Possessives

Possessive nouns are nouns (words that name a person, place, thing, or idea) that show ownership. Possessives are usually formed by adding *apostrophe* +s at the end of a noun. Have your child identify the words that are possessives in the list below. Then help your child find possessives in this book.

icicles	animal's	gifts	animals
clothes	New Year's	Valentine's	cards

CLOSE READING OF INFORMATIONAL TEXT

Close reading helps children comprehend text. It includes reading a text, discussing it with others, and answering questions about it. Use these questions to discuss this book with your child:

- Which season comes before winter?

- How might snow be a lot of work?

- What would you need in order to go ice skating?

- How is winter related to sleep?

- If you made up a song about winter, what would it sound like?

- Do you think winter is a good time of year or a bad time of year? Why do you think so?

FLUENCY

Fluency is the ability to read accurately with speed and expression. Help your child practice fluency by using one or more of the following activities:

- Reread this book to your child at least two times while he or she uses a finger to track each word as you read it.

- Read the first sentence aloud. Then have your child reread the sentence with you. Continue until you have finished this book.

- Ask your child to read aloud the words they know on each page of this book. (Your child will learn additional words with subsequent readings.)

- Have your child practice reading this book several times to improve accuracy, rate, and expression.

... Word List ...

Winter uses the 82 words listed below. *High-frequency* words are those words that are used most often in the English language. They are sometimes referred to as sight words because children need to learn to recognize them automatically when they read. *Content words* are any words specific to a particular topic. Regular practice reading these words will enhance your child's ability to read with greater fluency and comprehension.

High-Frequency Words

a	do	make	put	up
after	down	many	see	what
air	first	must	some	where
all	get(s)	new	the	will
and	give	not	their	work
another	go	now	there	year(s)
are	home	of	these	you
be	in	on	things	your
can	is	or	this	
come(s)	it	out	to	
day	like	people	too	

Content Words

animal(s, 's)	fun	leaves	snow(s)	try
cards	gifts	lot	snowman	Valentine
clothes	grow	play	special	wake
cold	hang	skating	spring	warm
fall	ice	sledding	stay	whoosh
frost	icicles	sleep	trees	winter

... About the Author

Mary Lindeen is a writer, editor, parent, and former elementary school teacher. She has written more than 100 books for children and edited many more. She specializes in early literacy instruction and books for young readers, especially nonfiction.

... About the Advisor

Dr. Shannon Cannon is a teacher educator in the School of Education at UC Davis, where she also earned her Ph.D. in Language, Literacy, and Culture. She serves on the clinical faculty, supervising pre-service teachers and teaching elementary methods courses in reading, effective teaching, and teacher action research.

DATE DUE

JAN 08 2018	
	PRINTED IN U.S.A.